ROSE HUMOUR

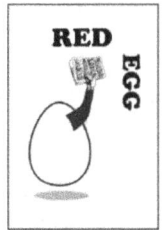

BY
MALCOLM DE CHAZAL

TRANSLATED BY
JEAN BONNIN

Rose Humour

An Original Publication of Red Egg Publishing

An imprint of Red Egg Publishing International

First published in the UK by Red Egg Publishing in 2022
www.redeggpublishing.com

Copyright © Jean Bonnin 2022

Jean Bonnin has asserted his moral right to be identified
as the author of this book, in the sense that
he is the translator

Cover design: J. Bonnin

British Library Cataloguing-in-Publication Data
A catalogue record for this book is available upon
request from the British Library
ISBN: 978-1-7397946-0-6

This book is sold subject to the condition that it shall not, by way of trade or otherwise, be lent, re-sold, hired out, or otherwise circulated without the publisher's prior consent in any form of binding or cover other than that in which it is published and without a similar condition including this condition being imposed on the subsequent purchaser.

ROSE HUMOUR

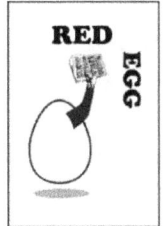

BY
MALCOLM DE CHAZAL

INTRODUCTION

Malcolm de Chazal (1902 – 1981) was born on the island of Mauritius. He was the thirteenth and last child… The de Chazal family had been French land-owning aristocracy. François de Chazal and Antoine-Toussaint de Chazal came to the island of Mauritius in 1763.

Malcolm de Chazal perceives the universe, spacetime, and spirituality in a distinct way that enables him to consider existence in a completely unique manner. Everything is part of the whole and everything exists in a fundamental state which is beyond mere consciousness. In his writing he coaxes us to consider the great quandaries. For us to be able to do this he helpfully provides us with definitions and insights to equip us with the necessary tools to analyse those big questions in the first instance. For he sees things we do not all have access to. Hence, he must provide us with a key so we can share in his visions. Even this key which he tantalisingly shares with us oftentimes requires us to approach our thought-processes from unfamiliar paths. A key for the key then? Not quite, but we must unburden ourselves from our modern-day tendencies to rationalise and analyse. We must begin to think the way Malcolm de Chazal thinks… and consequently see the way he sees.

Malcolm de Chazal is a surrealist and a mystic. For, indeed, surrealism and mysticism are states of mind as much as anything else. And in the case of de Chazal we experience that just out-of-reach of delineation dreamlike state so associated with the surrealists, which so uniquely merged with his transcendental approach to his writing and his life.
    Chazal's ethereality – in both his writing and his painting – can only truly be understood by seeing him as

being part of a long line of mystics and non-conforming thinkers. People whose views and approaches saw beyond the walls that so frequently create barriers to the comprehension of and immersion into the imagination.

François de Chazal was a confidante of the notorious Comte de St. Germaine, "A man who knows everything and who never dies", said Voltaire of the Comte. He might have added that he was a man whose origin was unknown and who disappeared without leaving a trace; and indeed, his great wealth was never satisfactorily explained either. And who, rumour had it, was a successful alchemist… Though he did on at least one occasion state that he was five hundred years old (which certainly could have been a reason for his having diamonds in his shoes which were supposedly worth in excess of 200,000 Francs); and when asked by Marie-Antoinette if he was going to settle in Paris, stated: "A century will pass before I come here again."

Of course, there has always been a fascination with the idea of living forever. The Hungarian Countess Erzsébet Báthory, for example, bathed in the blood of murdered virgins to try to infinitely prolong her life. The poet Charles Baudelaire left a suicide note, along with his failed 1845 attempt to kill himself. It read: "I'm killing myself because I believe I am immortal". And in 1869 the Comte de Lautréamont, whose real name was Isidore Lucien Ducasse, poet and strong influence upon the surrealists, wrote in his book Les Chants de Maldoror: immortality is the "terrifying problem that humanity has not yet solved."

Malcolm de Chazal, the poet, artist, and alchemist once stated that he was receiving very formidable premonitions of where his ancestor, le Comte François de Chazal de la Genesté, was buried. This was somewhat of a revelation since François' exact whereabouts were completely unknown. François de Chazal also, years before it happened, told of his presentiment that not only was there going to be a French Revolution, but that he also knew the details of what would transpire during those insurgent days to come.

François de Chazal, who was devoted to the occult, was such close friends with the Comte de St. Germaine that it is said he was the 'last depository' of the secrets of St. Germaine... François was known to be a practitioner of the art of *Lapis Animalis*, the transformation of stone into animals and visa versa, as well as the more common *Alchimia* or Alchemy, the changing of base metals into gold. François is also believed by many to have initiated the order of the very mysterious Rosicrucians.

As for Malcolm de Chazal himself, we can state that along this protracted line of mystery and intrigue he was its natural progeny. In the sense that he was also an alchemist; and he was a reclusive man, content to exist for a lot of the time in the spirituality of his inner mind. To a large extent he removed himself from society for, among other reasons, to try to create a completely new way of writing which bypassed rationale and the intellect, and instead channelled itself directly into the instinctive and the spiritual.

To appreciate the mystery and beauty that is Malcolm de Chazal one must look beyond the surface to that which is seemingly, if erroneously, tantalisingly just out of reach. But it is not. The inexplicable mystery and magnificence, and breathless wonderment are just there. If, like one of Marc Chagall's floating people, we reach up on tiptoe we will be able to grasp what Malcolm de Chazal calls: "La vie derrière les choses", life beyond the surface of [all] things. The immortality of breathless indivision, unseparateness, and the existence of gently gliding clouds within the sea and stars in the cliffs.

During the war years of 1939 to 1945 in Mauritius those with a philosophical focus, and the intellectuals more generally, would meet to discuss how things could be approached differently. It was during this period of debate and intense discussion and intellectual curiosity that Malcolm de Chazal developed or refined his perspective on breathed-in and experienced existence.

He became aware of the mythical continent of Lemuria where giants who sculpted the cliffs and the mountains resided. It was this enlightenment that helped to de-scale the eyes and comprehension for de Chazal. "I could no longer see my island with the same eye as before. A past had already welded me to the impossible", he stated.

In addition to this revelation was his experience in the gardens near his home. While taking in the air one day he spied an Azalea flower. This flower, stated de Chazal, was observing him, and he in turn looked at it... and it returned his gaze. "From now on", he wrote, "when I was nothing for men, for the flower *I was somebody*, since the flower took me into account... That's when it all becomes clear. The landscape in Mauritius was no longer cramped, only the men were". And, as he stated, because of these two experiences: "A new perspective opened up before me".

That perspective being that the mythology of time and time-history is superseded by the experience that the now-ness of *being* is part of the interconnectedness of legend. And it is solely a profound comprehension of mythology – and that the fluidity of inanimacy is interchangeable and indistinguishable – that is vital. Essentially that the divisions are sculpted from thin-air out of insubstantiality, and in truth we (and in this discussion de Chazal's island) have a story which dates back to the beginning of time – and this story is the story of the inseparability of existence and magic.

Malcolm de Chazal was an alchemist and a visionary who saw the magic in everything and the legend all around us. There are no barriers he tells us and the sooner we truly grasp this the sooner we can strive forward to the realm where words are surpassed by thought, and thought, in turn, by the whirlpool of interconnectedness that de Chazal signals to us results in understanding.

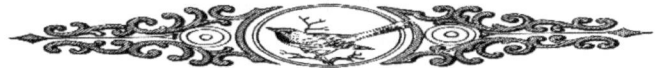

According to Christopher Montemayor in his essay on *The Evolution of Surrealism*, the surrealists had an "obsession with mystery". This is in no small part due to what Albert Camus describes as: the antithesis with anything which could not be called surrealistic. Namely, that "surrealism's essential enemy is rationalism".

"The Surrealist revolution had this incalculable advantage of bringing the irrational into everyday life and of having made known to men the treasures of the unconscious... Poetry thus has an end. The absolute liberation of man". Malcolm de Chazal, 1960...

For a greater understanding of Malcolm de Chazal's insights and approach we recommend his two books:
Magical Sense – ISBN 978-0-9571258-6-5
Magical Science – ISBN 978-0-9571258-7-2

"The flower in the vase smiles, but no longer laughs".

"Monkeys are superior to men in this:
when a monkey looks into a mirror, he sees a monkey".

"Art is nature speeded up and God slowed down".

"The light played leapfrog with the shadows.
Its last leap was into this bouquet of roses
Where it was crushed into shards".

Malcolm de Chazal

1.

The Peacock
Is itself
A rainbow

2.

When the knockout
Came
The man
Felt
He was
Boxing himself

3.

Charm
Is endless
Sensual
Delight

4.

A baby's
Mouth
Is its
First bonbon

5.

All accidents
Happen
When
The road
Changes
Its Mind

6.

'No'
Always
Opposes
'Yes'
Except
In financial
Affaires

7.

The wound
Laughed
In
Pain

8.

Without leaves
Flowers
Become
Myopic

9.

The mattress
Awaited
The man
In order
To sleep

10.

Logic
Is unable
To accept
Reason

11.

His body
Was
In fashion

12.

He was
Considered
Stupid
Because
He had
Arrived at the
Very end
Of his thoughts

13.

Each bird
Is the colour
Of its
Call

14.

Whisky
Was drunk :
Man
Drank it
Badly

15.

He was
So stubborn
He opposed
Himself

16.

The green beans
Made
The plate
Jump

17.

The
Egg
Is
Chiny
Chin

18.

Water in a
Vase
Never
Rises above
Its kidneys

19.

The sorcerer
Is
Well-done
When
He
Himself
Is
Bewitched

20.

Time
Only counts
For people
Who are
Slow

21.

Water
In the
Dyke
Moves
Like
A
Hippopotamus

22.

She orchestrated
Her silence
Then
Began
To sing

23.

Green
Is the
Warmth
Of Spring
And the
Cool
Of summer

24.

The bird
Which
Is afraid
Feels
Caged

25.

A record
Spinning
At an
Infinite
Speed
Enables
The arm
To pass
Through

26.

Breath
Sings
When it
Is kissing

27.

The separation
Of the buttocks
Is a
Double
Apostrophe

28.

Maternity
Creates
Another
Mouth

29.

Sensual people
Eat the dessert
Before
The soup

30.

Of all of
Our
Body parts
It is
The tongue
Which is
The most
familiar
To us

31.

Wind
Is winded
When
It is
Slapped

32.

Blotting paper
Is the same
In any
Language

33.

Shadow
Is the
Portal
Of space

34.

The bottle
Was
Always
Beside
Itself

35.

Every
Pebble
That
Falls
Appears
Unstuck

36.

The wave
Senses
The boat
Yet the boat
Cannot
Sense
The wave

37.

As it
Ate
The mouth
Was
Astride

38.

The
Ossuaries
Are
Tombollas

39.

Gold is
The metal
With
The broadest
Shoulders

40.

The last
Sensation
Of suspension
Is what
Wrenches
The feet

41.

His gaze
Was
Spring-like

42.

Moonlight
Dances
In Circles

43.

Fur
Silk
Satin
Lace
Wool
Cotton
Can all
Be found
In the
Body
Of a
Woman

44.

The Plantigrades
Arrived
When man
Behaved
As if
He was
A quadruped

45.

The gaze
Awaited
As an
Accent
Circumflex

46.

Sourness
Is an
Embalmed
Taste

47.

The eye
Of the flower
Does not
Look
Around itself
To give enough
Space
To its
Leaves

48.

The pillow
Always had
A sour face
The sheet
Was always
Good-humoured

49.

She
Masturbated
In
Credit

50.

The wind
Dropped
Its hand
To be
Kissed
By the
Bubbling
Spring

51.

Water
Drops
Her skirt
When
The oar
Passes by

52.

He made
His
Recollections
More
Youthful
In his
Imagination

53.

The sun
Placed
A watchstrap
Around
The moon

54.

Light sleeps
Standing up
And
Night sleeps
All ways at once

55.

All animals
Smile
When
They
Drink

56.

In mud
Light
Has colic

57.

Summer
Is soaked up
By the
Rain

58.

The hip
Is the verb
In the conversation
Of dresses

59.

The meter
Was astonished
That no one
Could
Understand
Its
Length

60.

Blue
Was pale
With joy.
It was
Springtime

61.

The
Vegetables
Were
Eating
Their soup
In the broth

62.

The
Runny omelette
Drooled
With
Hunger

63.

Wire
Is
A line
Of
Rupture

64.

The crucified
Converted

65.

The
Bread
We were
Toasting
Crunched
Its
Dough

66.

Sourness
Only
Throws
Up
When
Alone

67.

The bourgeoisie
Have never
Succeeded
In gentrifying
Their
Chamber pots

68.

The ball
Massaged
Itself

69.

The
Water cascaded
Believing
It was
In a
Boat

70.

In order
To warm
Up
Tiredness
Began
To
Run

71.

The enriched
Quantity
Covered itself
In
Qualities

72.

The
Full bottle
Drank
Its litre

73.

The glove
Caught
The hand
When
Put on

74.

The oversewn
Dress
Hung
Itself
Up

75.

The carrot
On
The plate
Had
Lost
Its nose

76.

The fire
Was aggrieved
Because
The wood
Didn't
Understand it

77.

The boutique
Bought
So much
From itself
That it
Never
Saw another
Client

78.

The bill
Did
Its
Accounts

79.

She had
Some
Sensible
Footsteps
In her
Foolish
Feet

80.

She
Cut out
Her dresses
From
Absent fabric

81.

The unfaithful
Ring
Was divorced from
Its
Decisions

82.

The dye
Made
Itself up
With rouge
And
Became
Pale

83.

The first
Shoemaker
Is the
Spine
Of the
Fish

84.

The dust
Tired
Of
Dusting itself
Let its
Brush
Fall

85.

The dislike
Of colour
Vanished
Among
The bedsheets

86.

With his
Subterranean eye
The sewer
Looked
At the cave
Which made
The sewer
Avert
Its gaze

87.

The only
Key
To space
Is
Observation

88.

Traitors
Never
Pay heed
To
Turncoats

89.

There
Is no
Element
Of chance
To being
A genius

90.

Rain
Loosened
Its seatbelt
In the
Turning
Of the
Wave

91.

The kiss
Is the
Breast
That
Suckles

92.

Thunder
Is the
Cry
Of Anguish
Of fire

93.

The horizon
Never
Takes
An unnecessary
Step

94.

When the
Saint arrived
At the
Feast
Of Eternity
He'd found
He's lost
His appetite

95.

Not having
Pretty hands
She expanded
Them
With rings

96.

The bridge
No longer
Remembered
Which end
Was its
Present
And which
Its past

97.

True love
Has wounds
That
Never
Bleed

98.

Virgins
Are always
Eaten up
The first time
After which
It is they
Who do
The devouring

99.

The cork
Uncorked
Caught a cold
From
The smell

100.

His steps
Floated
Him
Onwards

101.

The beaten
Iron
Stuttered
Its
Beaten
Sentiments

102.

The table
Was turning.
All the women
Around
Were
Wearing
The same
Dress

103.

"Table"
As a word
Never has
The same
Shape

104.

The eye
Of the needle
Lost the
Thread
Of its
Ideas

105.

The steak
Didn't
Like
Veal

106.

Wine
Finds its
True taste
While
Being
Drunk

107.

Converted morality
Becomes
The
Law

108.

The dress
Sneezed
Into
Its
Ruffles

109.

Violence
Cried
Over
The debris
Of tenderness

110.

The fog
Is an
Umbrella
Without
Ribbing

111.

Breath
Is always
Fearful
Of being
Swallowed up

112.

The river
Flows
Décolleté
In its
Bed

113.

Marriage
Is a guarantee
Against
Virginity

114.

The cockerel
Removed
His teeth
When he pecked
And he put them
Back in
When he crowed

115.

The regiment
Raised
Its eyebrows
At every
Bugle blast

116.

Weight
Only feels
Strong
When on
The scales

117.

Gold
Is enriched
When its
Next
To a pearl
But diminished
When next
To a
Diamond

NOTES AND ACKNOWLEDGEMENTS

Thanks to: Lyn Bonnin, A.P. Mousnier, and Robert Furlong.

Other books by Jean Bonnin:

Novels
A Certain Experience of the Impossible – ISBN: 978-1-906174-07-3
The Cubist's House – ISBN: 978-0957125858
Lines Within the Circle – ISBN: 978-0957125803

Poetry/Aphorisms
Being and Somethingness – ISBN: 978-0957125834
Beautiful Wilderness – ISBN: 978-0957125889
Dreams Within Dreams – ISBN: 978-1999821517

Translations
Magical Sense (by Malcolm de Chazal) – ISBN: 978-0957125865
Magical Science (by Malcolm de Chazal) – ISBN: 978-0957125872

Edited by Jean Bonnin
The Nuremberg Trials: A Personal History (by Georges Bonnin)
ISBN: 978-0957125841

In French
Sense Magique by Malcolm de Chazal (with an Introduction by Jean Bonnin) ISBN: 978-1-9998215-3-1

Artwork and Art History
Surrealism In Wales – ISBN: 978-1-9998215-4-8
Surrealism in Wales: Artworks and Images – ISBN: 978-1-9998215-5-5
A Guidebook to Surrealism: Surrealism by Surrealists – ISBN: 978-1-7397946-1-3